THE
FIRST WOMAN
IN
CONGRESS:
Jeannette Rankin

by Judy Rachel Block

Illustrated by
Terry Kovalcik

cpi

contemporary perspectives, inc.

This book is distributed by Silver Burdett Company, Morristown, New Jersey, 07960.

Library of Congress Number: 78-14490

Art and Photo Credits

Cover illustration, Terry Kovalcik
Photo on page 13, courtesy of The Museum of the American Indian, Heye Foundation
Photos on pages 29, 30, 41, and 48, Photoworld
Photo on page 33, courtesy of The League of Women Voters
Photos on pages 39, 42, and 44, Culver Pictures
Every effort has been made to trace the ownership of all copyrighted material in this book and to obtain permission for its use.

Library of Congress Cataloging in Publication Data

Block, Judith Rachel, 1948-
    The first woman in Congress: Jeannette Rankin

    SUMMARY: Traces the career of the first woman to hold a congressional office.
    1. Rankin, Jeannette. 2. Legislators — United States — Biography — Juvenile literature. 3. Women in politics — United States — Biography — Juvenile literature. [1. Rankin, Jeannette. 2. Legislators. 3. Women in politics] I. Title
JK1030.R3B56   328.73′092′4   [B] [92]   78-14490
ISBN 0-89547-053-5

Manufactured in the United States of America
ISBN 0-89547-053-5

Contents

Chapter 1

Alone

Jeannette Rankin was up early on the morning of December 8, 1941. She was surprised at not feeling more tired. Congresswoman Rankin had slept very little the night before. And no wonder. Japanese airplanes had attacked Pearl Harbor, Hawaii, less than 24 hours ago.

President Franklin D. Roosevelt had asked Congress to meet today. It would be one of the most important meetings in their stormy history. Jeannette Rankin had a lot of thinking to do before this meeting.

President Roosevelt, starting his third term, had told Congress about the bombing of American ships and planes by the Japanese. The president called it "an act of war," in a voice shaking with anger. Many Americans had been killed or hurt. Now, he said, there was nothing for Congress to do but vote for war against Japan.

But for Jeannette Rankin, congresswoman from the state of Montana — the first woman ever in the House of Representatives — a vote for war was not easy. For the second time in her life she suddenly felt all alone. She had had to make this choice before, and then it had seemed like the hardest choice she had ever made. This time it seemed *impossible*.

As she sat in the darkness of her living room that morning, the congresswoman felt her eyes filling with tears. She watched the shadows of dancing tree branches move back and forth on the wall. Listening to the icy wind running across her window, she thought back to that first difficult time 24 years ago.

"Congresswoman Rankin. How do you vote? Yes or no?" It was the Speaker of the House — Representative Champ Clark of Missouri — asking the question. His words went right to Jeannette Rankin's heart. They were like cold fingers moving down her spine.

The moment she had feared was finally here. The year was 1917. Most of the world was at war. And now the U.S. House of Representatives was about to vote America into World War I. The senators had already spoken. They had voted to go to war against Germany. In a few minutes peace would only be a memory.

But Jeannette Rankin strongly believed that war was the wrong thing for her country. She thought war was wrong — any time, any place. She could not see how killing and fighting could ever solve the world's problems. But she also knew America's friends needed help now more than ever before. How could she vote to keep the United States out of World War I?

"Congresswoman Rankin!" Once again the Speaker called her name. "We are all waiting for your vote."

The 37-year-old congresswoman took a deep breath as she stood by her chair. She looked out over the crowded room. The eyes of every congressman were on her. She looked up at the visitors sitting in the gallery. They too sat staring at her, waiting for her

vote. There was not a sound in the great hall. And then Jeannette Rankin spoke.

"I want to stand by my country. I want to help our friends in Europe. But I cannot vote for war. I vote . . . no!"

Her words struck like a clap of thunder in the historic chamber. Few congressmen could believe what they had just heard. Jeannette Rankin had turned away from her own country when it needed her most! She had heard President Woodrow Wilson say that only America could "make the world safe for democracy." Still, she had voted against going to war.

Jeannette took her seat. Her lips and knees shook. She waited for the final vote. She was not alone in her stand against the war. Eight congressmen voted along with her. And two days earlier, six senators had also voted against the U.S. entering the war. But these few voices could not change what was to come. When the votes were counted, the country was at war with Germany. America would send its soldiers to fight on the battlefields of Europe!

Jeannette Rankin's vote on April 6, 1917, against entering World War I, was a great act of courage. She had gone against the advice of her own family and many close friends. She had gone against President Wilson's own strong feelings. But she did not believe that war was the only way to keep freedom for the world.

So Jeannette Rankin had made the difficult decision to follow her own hard-won beliefs. This would have been unusual for anyone at any time. But in 1917, it was a historic moment. For Jeannette Rankin was the first woman ever to be elected to the U.S. Congress.

In a sense, when she voted no, she was speaking for women everywhere. The eyes of every man and woman in the country were on her. And there she was — the first and only woman with the chance to stand up for peace and vote in the U.S. Congress against war.

At the time Jeannette Rankin was born, a woman could not become a member of Congress. A woman could not even vote in a general election in her home state. Jeannette Rankin and other women changed all this after winning many long, hard battles over the years.

But why does someone come to believe so strongly that war is wrong? Jeannette Rankin's belief in peace was even stronger than her desire to be a congresswoman. It all began when she was a young child. She developed her strength of character because her family and home life were different from most of her neighbors'.

Chapter 2

Growing Up on the Montana Frontier

Jeannette Rankin was born on June 11, 1880, in the small pioneer town of Missoula, Montana. When she was young, Montana was also young — a part of the western frontier. Jeannette grew up in the age of real cowboys and Indians, settlers and copper miners. She knew the West of wild animals and wide-open blue skies. In fact, Montana was, and still is, known as the Big Sky Country.

One cold winter night when Jeannette was still quite young, she and her family huddled around a warm crackling fire. It was the perfect night to hear an exciting story about the Old West. Her father, John

Rankin, had entertained his six children with such stories many times before.

There was nothing odd about the children gathering around him this night. But the story he would tell tonight was special. It was one he hoped his children would never forget.

Mr. Rankin would tell his family the story of Chief Joseph and the Nez Percé Indians. The Rankins would learn about the Nez Percé's trip across Montana. And about an awful war that ended only because of the good heart of their leader — Chief Joseph.

"Chief Joseph was a peaceful and noble American Indian," John Rankin began. "His trouble started when he led his people away from their home — a reservation in Idaho. He was leading them to Canada. He hoped they would find a better life there.

"The Nez Percé tribe reached the Montana Territory. The land and its people were protected by U.S. soldiers. They didn't believe Chief Joseph when he told them why his tribe was on the move. Nor did they believe him when he promised that his people wanted no trouble — no shooting or bloodshed. The soldiers asked the Nez Percé to give up all their guns. They would not let them cross Montana to Canada unless they did."

CHIEF JOSEH
COPYRIGHT 1901.
LEE MOORHOUSE

"But Father, how could the Indians give up their guns?" Jeannette Rankin had broken into her father's story. She was the oldest of the six Rankin children. "They would have no way of hunting deer and buffalo for food. They would surely die of hunger."

Her father smiled at the question. "That's just what Chief Joseph told the commander of the soldiers," answered John Rankin quietly. "But again the army men would not believe him. To be sure they would have no trouble with Chief Joseph's people, the U.S. Army actually planned to kill every last one of the Nez Percé Indians in Montana. 'Before they kill *us*,' said the officers in charge."

John Rankin's voice rose in anger as he talked about the army's awful plan. It was hard for him to tell his story without feeling ill. But he went on. He felt it was important that his children know just what happened that day in 1877.

"The soldiers sent word to all the white people in the Montana Territory. They were to bring guns to Lolo Pass. They knew that Chief Joseph would have to lead his people through the pass on his way to Canada. So they laid a trap for them there. No Indian would be allowed through unless his gun was given up to the army. If the Nez Percé Indians put up a fight, every man, woman, and child in the tribe would be killed!"

Jeannette and the other children cringed as they heard their father tell of the soldiers' plan. This time Wellington, Jeannette's only brother, broke in.

"How could American soldiers kill hundreds of other Americans, Father? How could they ever live with themselves after that?"

"There are many people who think that killing is the only way to settle a tough problem," his father answered. There was sadness in his voice. "They won't even give peaceful answers a *try*. But Chief Joseph was smart enough to know that these soldiers thought in this narrow-minded way.

"So in the dead of night, he led his people *around* the soldiers' trap. The Nez Percé Indians escaped into the high mountain country. If Chief Joseph hadn't outsmarted the soldiers, the whole tribe might have been slaughtered!"

John Rankin stopped talking. The children seemed to understand why he had told them this story. Their father had seen too much killing in his day. And no matter how hard it was, he had to teach them that war and killing were wrong.

Because of her father's strong feelings, Jeannette Rankin grew up believing that war was totally wrong.

This belief would never leave her. Later, she would carry these strong feelings against war all the way to the U.S. Congress.

Jeannette Rankin's childhood in Montana made her believe she could do anything she put her mind to. She saw the women of the Old West working right alongside their men. Together they built homes in the wilderness and plowed the fields for planting.

These strong pioneer women taught Jeannette how important it is to be strong — in body and in the will to work hard. They taught her it was important to be strong of both mind and purpose. Most of all, they taught her to take great pride in being a woman.

Jeannette had four younger sisters and one younger brother. They all lived with their parents and went to school in the town of Missoula for most of the year. But the short Montana summers were spent on the family ranch six miles outside of town.

Summers at the ranch were Jeannette's happiest times. At the ranch she found answers to the problems of everyday life on the frontier. She learned how to fix a plow, put down a wooden sidewalk, milk the cows, and care for animals.

But her summers at the ranch taught her something even more important. They taught her to take chances on her own ideas about how to do things. She had to learn new skills. And she had to use them. She learned to believe in herself — in her own abilities and in her dreams.

Jeannette Rankin lived with her family until she finished college at the age of 22. Most of her friends were now married. But Jeannette had different ideas. She did not want to marry. She wanted to see something of the world outside Montana. And she would do it on her own. She wanted no help from her family, her friends, or from anyone.

After college, Jeannette tried to figure out what she wanted from life. She tried nursing, teaching, and furniture design. Nothing seemed right for her. John Rankin encouraged his daughter to keep searching. He was sure she would find work that would have real meaning for her. His support was always there for Jeannette.

Then suddenly, in 1904, John Rankin died. Jeannette felt the loss deeply — not only because her father was gone, but because he had been such a good friend. He had been the strongest influence in her life. She never forgot his ideas against war.

She wanted to be with her brother Wellington now. But he was studying law in Boston, Massachusetts.

Well, she wanted to see more of the country. Here was her chance.

Jeannette's trip to Boston took her to the East for the first time in her life. And for the first time, she saw life in the big city. There she found what she was looking for. She saw the homes and neighborhoods of poor people. She saw wasted lives that seemed without any hope. She saw young children living in miserable slums.

These people badly needed some help. Now Jeannette knew what she wanted. She would spend her life helping those who needed her — those who had no one else to turn to. She would become a social worker!

Jeannette Rankin went to the other end of the country — to San Francisco, California. There she trained to be a social worker. After that, her future seemed clear. She never dreamed that social work would only be a stepping-stone. Another more important career lay just beyond it.

And Jeannette Rankin never would have dreamed that she would soon be in the thick of a battle that had been taking shape in America for many years. It was a battle that would change the rest of her life.

Chapter 3

Women Must Vote!

Jeannette Rankin's first job as a social worker was in Spokane, Washington. And in that city she found *more* than she was looking for. She met many women who were working hard to get women the right to vote.

To the young social worker's surprise, she had never thought too much about the American government or how it worked. Now she was finding and joining groups of women who had done a lot of thinking about the way their country was run. And they were not happy about it.

Jeannette Rankin found out that America had been run by the votes of men for over 100 years. Women were going to have to fight for what was right. Women had to join the battle for the vote. And that battle would have to be won in every state across the country.

21

Jeannette spoke to people on Spokane street corners. Day after day, she handed out posters and leaflets. She spoke at meetings and met with new groups of women all over the state. She joined marches to the state capital in Seattle. And in time, the women of Washington *did* win the right to vote in state and local elections.

Jeannette was overjoyed. She felt that for the first time in her life she had done something really important for others. And she knew that she had to go back to her home state of Montana. She had to help bring about the same rights for women there. Nothing was more important to her than helping the women of Montana get the vote. And after this first victory in the state of Washington, nothing about her life would ever be the same again.

"I just can't stand by while they laugh at us," said Jeannette. Her face was red with anger. "This is 1910. We're living in modern times. Women have to stand on their own and be counted. To do that, we must have the right to vote!"

"I agree with you," answered her brother Wellington. He was trying to calm his sister down. They had had this talk many times. "But so far, the Montana state senators won't listen. The women's voting bill has been before them since 1902. That's eight years, and they still make a joke of it every time

it comes up. To them, the women's vote just isn't important."

"*Nothing* is more important than equal voting rights," said Jeannette. "Women built Montana along with men. They must also be able to vote along with men!"

"You can tell me that all day. But it won't do any good," said Wellington. "This is not the state of Washington. There are no women's groups here yet. If you want the vote in Montana, you'll have to lead the fight here yourself!"

Wellington's ringing words took his older sister by surprise. Jeannette had never started a fight for women's voting rights on her own. Someone else had always taken the lead. But here, in her home state of Montana, it seemed there *was* no one else. Jeannette stuck her chin out firmly as she answered her brother.

"I'll ask to speak before the state House of Representatives. I'll tell them why women must be given the vote. They'll never turn women's rights into a joke again!"

Jeannette was not nervous until she walked into the state House chamber. There, row upon row of men were waiting to hear her speak. To her surprise, most

stood up and clapped loudly as she walked to the front to speak.

"Gentlemen," began Jeannette. Her voice shook as she began. "I have come to ask you to give women the vote. We have shared your struggle to build Montana. Now we must share in the vote!"

With each word, Jeannette's voice grew stronger. She had to make these men change their minds. If she failed, it would be years before Montana women would vote.

There was no laughter when Jeannette Rankin finished speaking. There was no sound at all. The Montana representatives had never been given such strong reasons for passing a bill. When the room suddenly filled with the cheers of men, Jeannette was thrilled. Not that she had won the battle — that would take a long time. The bill would have to pass. Then all the men of Montana would have to vote on it. But at least the women's vote was no longer a joke.

The Montana representatives were not quite ready to give voting rights to women even after Miss Rankin's talk. The voting amendment missed by only a few votes this time. And women's groups were now springing up in every part of Montana. They had heard the call and were ready to fight for their rights.

Chapter 4

Women Fight for the Vote

Women across the country heard the voice first raised in Montana. They had another leader. Jeannette Rankin's help was asked for by women everywhere. She talked on street corners in New York City. She talked in union halls of Ohio. She talked to anyone who would listen. She marched, carrying posters, in the towns and villages of Wisconsin. By 1912 Jeannette was a leader among American women who wanted to vote. And she had been working for the right to vote for only two years!

Now Jeannette and other leaders of the vote movement were growing much stronger. They had won the vote in many states. It was time to take on the president and the Congress of the United States.

Women in the voting rights movement wanted Congress to pass an amendment to the U.S.

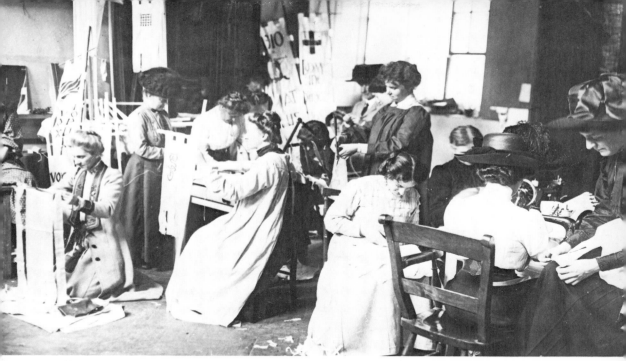

Women's groups around the country made posters for their voting marches.

Constitution. It would give *all* American women the right to vote. This amendment would then become law for the whole country once three-fourths of the states agreed to it. Jeannette and her friends believed that this would be faster than starting the fight over again in every single state. Still, to be on the safe side, they continued to work hard to change state voting laws as well.

The women decided to show everyone how many people were behind them. On March 4, 1913, a new president was to be sworn in. His name was Woodrow Wilson. Women from all over the country came to Washington on March 3. Their plan was to greet President Wilson with a huge parade through the city.

The new president had to understand that the women's right to vote should be his most important goal.

On the day of the parade, Jeannette took her place in line. She looked around at the hundreds of women there with her. All were giving their time and energy to the women's voting movement. And Jeannette Rankin was proud. She was sure that today would be their greatest day. But her dream was about to be suddenly shattered.

"Look out, Jeannette," yelled a woman standing in line. "Duck!"

Jeannette ducked just in time. A burning cigar stub whizzed by. It missed her head by inches.

"Get back in the kitchen where you belong," shouted an angry man in the crowd.

"No vote for women!" yelled another.

Jeannette could not understand what had happened. A crowd of men had turned against the women. The men were pushing their way into the street, blocking the parade. They were pushing some of the women around and shouting loud insults.

"Where are the police?" Jeannette called out.

"They're here," answered one frightened woman. She pointed to a group of policemen. "But they aren't doing anything to stop this!"

The police were on the side of the angry men in the crowd! Jeannette Rankin knew now that the fight would be a long and bitter one. A parade, even a new president, was not going to be all that was needed. *Very well then. She would work that much harder!*

And she did. She went home — back to Montana. There she formed more women's voting groups. She spoke in every town that asked for her. After months of hard work, Jeannette finally won.

It was 1913. There were only two votes against the women's amendment. Now it was all in the hands of Montana's voters — the men!

Women all around the country joined in the movement for voting rights. There were women marching in every U.S. city.

Jeannette Rankin went from one corner of the state to the other. This time she was talking to men's groups. And she did not simply tell them how much the women of Montana had done to help the men build the state. She made them understand how much more voting power this would give them. If a man could show his wife good reasons for voting his way, her vote would add to his.

Jeannette Rankin was smart. She was showing the men how they could be helped by women voters. The message worked with many labor unions and working-men's clubs.

All her hard work was rewarded on Election Day. The votes were counted. The men of Montana gave the women the vote at last! In a way Jeannette Rankin felt that this was *her* victory. And many others felt the same way. She had worked harder than anyone else for the amendment. Only the governor was more famous than Jeannette Rankin in Montana.

But now Miss Rankin had to think about what she would do next with her life. She wanted to go on helping the people of Montana — men and women alike. She wanted to help the poor and those who could not help themselves. But how?

Once again she talked with her brother Wellington. And once again he proved to be the friend she thought she lost when her father died. But what she heard her brother say came as a great surprise. She was not sure she could believe what he had just said. He saw her look of shock. So he said it again.

"You heard me, Jeannette. You are about the best known name and face in the state. I know it has never been done by a women, but maybe the time has come to try it. Run for the United States Congress. Run. And I bet you'll win!"

Chapter 5

Jeannette Rankin Goes to Washington

The year was 1916. The July day was hot and dry. The summer sun of Montana was bright in a cloudless sky. Jeannette Rankin slowly climbed the long steps of the courthouse in Missoula, Montana. She was home again. And again she was going to talk to the people. She reached the top and turned to face the crowd. Her brother Wellington was among them.

"I would like to make an announcement. I am entering the race for the United States Congress." The words hit people like a giant electric shock. But they could see this tough 36-year-old woman meant every word she was saying. "I was born in Montana. I have

grown up here. I know what matters to you, its people.
Please elect me as your congresswoman. I promise to
make your ideals of peace and equal rights the law of
the land."

Over the next few months, Jeannette Rankin
spoke to copper miners, lumberjacks, mothers, and
bank clerks. At each stop she explained what she stood
for. She told the people why they should send her to
Congress.

"I stand for peace," said Jeannette in a strong voice.
She was speaking to a roomful of copper miners. "If
you elect me as your congresswoman, I promise to do
everything I can to keep the United States out of war."

The miners looked at each other and nodded. Strong
words, but did she mean it? "She gets my vote if she
can do that!" one of them said in a voice loud enough
for all to hear.

War was on everyone's mind in Montana. People
spoke out about it all the time. A terrible war was
going on in Europe. Montana voters did not want the
United States to get mixed up in it. They did not want
their sons to die in a "European problem."

"I will also work for laws that protect the rights of
children," Jeannette continued. "And I will help to
pass a national law giving women the right to vote."

Jeannette's words seemed to uplift everyone who heard them. But she was worried. Would it matter that the words were spoken by a woman? Could the people of her state believe that she could be a voice for them in Washington, D. C.?

Jeannette was up before dawn on November 16, 1916. She was too excited to eat breakfast. What happened on this day would tell the story of the rest of her life.

It was Election Day, and she would know by evening if she was headed for Washington, D. C. But this day was special for still another reason. Today Jeannette Rankin, along with countless other women, would vote for the first time in her life!

When the statewide votes were counted, she could hardly believe what had happened. She had won by over 7,000 votes! She would sit in the U.S. House of Representatives! The little girl from Missoula had become America's first congresswoman.

Congresswoman Rankin came to Washington, D.C. in April 1917. The times could not have been worse. The call to war was on everyone's lips. German submarines had sunk ships carrying U.S. citizens. This clearly put America in danger. President Wilson felt he had no choice. Even with his own feelings against war he asked the Congress to declare war on Germany.

Representative Jeannette Rankin makes her first speech in the U.S. Congress.

The vote on the president's call to war would be Jeannette's first important vote in Congress. And it would take place only four days after she was sworn in to office! She had to do the right thing. She had to — for herself, for Montana, and for all the women of America. She remembered her father's belief that war was the wrong way to solve problems.

Friends she had known for years tried to talk Jeannette into voting for the war. Her brother Wellington felt the same way. "Jeannette, you've got to vote for war," Wellington pleaded. "You'll ruin your chances to be elected again if you vote against the war."

"My vote will have nothing to do with getting elected again," answered Jeannette. She was disappointed in Wellington. Could her reelection be more important to him than the lives of American soldiers? "I could never live with myself if I voted to send young men to war just to save my job."

Wellington's and Jeannette's friends were not the only ones who tried to make her vote for war. Many of the women who fought with her for women's rights also wanted her to vote yes. Some thought that if a woman voted against the war the cause of women would be set back throughout the country. They were afraid people would think that women could not make tough choices in Congress.

Representative Jeannette Rankin, the first U.S. congresswoman, around the time of her election.

If women were ever to be elected again, Jeannette would have to vote for war just like a man. But as always, Jeannette made up her own mind. It didn't matter what others might say.

Jeannette Rankin cast her vote *against* the war on April 6, 1917. She disappointed many people, but she was true to herself.

Jeannette worked night and day to make life better for the people of Montana. But her brother Wellington had been right. Montana voters could not accept her stand against the war. And in March 1919, Jeannette Rankin left Congress. She had not been reelected.

President Woodrow Wilson asks the U.S. Congress to declare war on Germany.

Over the next 20 years, Jeannette never stopped working for the cause of peace. She joined all groups trying to find a way to peace in a troubled world. She received help and thanks from people all over the country. But she wanted, most of all, to have her seat in Congress again.

In 1939 she ran for that seat. And for the second time, she won! But just as before, the dark clouds of war raced across Europe. And everyone was sure America would finally have to get involved. What would she do if she had to decide again to vote yes or no on America's going to war?

Chapter 6

Chief Joseph Lives Again

Congresswoman Jeannette Rankin, age 61, snapped out of her daydream. She had work to do. The past was past. She had to live in the present. But she had the feeling that she was about to relive the most important day of her life. And both of them had taken place in the U.S. Congress! The great powers of Europe and the Pacific were already fighting.

In 1917 there had been a few brave people who had agreed with Jeannette's vote against World War I. But now, in 1941, it seemed as if everyone in the country wanted to fight Japan and Germany in World War II. The people wanted war. The press wanted war. So did Congress. Jeannette asked herself, "What do *I* want?" The time had come to answer that question. She

President Roosevelt tells Congress that Japanese airplanes have attacked Pearl Harbor, Hawaii.

walked briskly out of her Washington house, hailed a cab, and went to the Capitol building — "the hill," as the congressional meeting place is called.

Talks had begun by the time she got to her seat in the House of Representatives. Jeannette Rankin now knew what she would do. Her mind was made up. She raised her hand to speak. The Speaker of the House, Congressman Sam Rayburn, looked her way. "Mr. Speaker, . . . Mr. Speaker!" she called.

"You're out of order, Congresswoman Rankin."

"Mr. Speaker, I would like to be heard," cried Jeannette once more. Again and again she rose, trying to get a chance to speak. But each time she was told to sit down.

Finally the talk ended. Jeannette never got an opportunity to speak her mind. It was time to vote. The names of all the members of Congress were called in turn. One by one, each congressman cast a vote for war. Not one congressman would even talk against the war. And one congresswoman, Jeannette Rankin, knew that the president had no choice but to feel as he did. She knew what she had to do now.

"Congresswoman Rankin," called the Speaker. "How do you vote?"

"I vote *NO!*" answered Jeannette Rankin. Her voice was loud and clear. "As a woman, I cannot go to war. And I refuse to send anyone else!"

"Traitor!" yelled a voice from the crowd.

"Women don't belong in Congress," called another.

These harsh words stung Jeannette like a whip. Then she suddenly thought of her father's story of many years ago — about Chief Joseph and the Nez Percé Indians. She remembered the look on her father's face when he told her what Chief Joseph said to the soldiers: "I will fight no more forever!"

Jeannette's heart soared with hope. What more could she want than to offer Chief Joseph's hopes for peace to her country?

Chapter 7

A Final Word

When the vote in Congress was counted that day in 1941, there were 388 votes for war and one vote against war. Jeannette Rankin had truly stood alone. She was cursed and shunned by even her closest friends.

She spoke out against war to the very end of her life. Few would even listen. But then, on June 11, 1970, she was honored by the Congress of the United States. She finally took her reward for bravery as one of the first "doves of peace."

Jeannette Rankin died May 18, 1973. She was 92. She is perhaps best remembered in the words of a

Jeannette Rankin receives a Hall of Fame Susan B. Anthony award at the age of 90. Susan B. Anthony was a leader of the women's voting movement between 1869 and 1900.

U.S. Senator who later became president. John F. Kennedy, in 1958, said of America's first woman in Congress ... *She was one of the most fearless people in American history ...*